May I Come In?

Divya Narayanan

BookLeaf Publishing

India | USA | UK

Presentation by *BookLeaf Publishing*

Web: www.bookleafpub.com

E-mail: info@bookleafpub.com

ISBN: 9789360941802

First edition 2024

DEDICATION

I dedicate this work to myself, for showing up, trying through, and completing what I intended to. I dedicate this book to my younger self who once dreamt of being an author, and to the woman I have become, through this journey of life. I dedicate this book to all those life-partners who knows nothing else but to love and support their best halves in whatever they do. I dedicate this to all children who look up to their parents as their real-life heroes. I dedicate this to all those who are waiting for that "extra time", to accomplish things that they truly love.

ACKNOWLEDGEMENT

I thank every visible and invisible soul in my journey without whom I would not be here now to create this piece of work. I thank the Supreme power and my Guru parampara, (lineage) without whose blessings this would not have been possible. I thank my family, who have always believed in me and have been the strongest pillar of support. I sincerely thank the publisher for extending their name to support my journey.

PREFACE

Each poem in this book is a reflection of the author's views about elements that are a part of everyday life. She uses simple language to get her thoughts across and tries to remind the readers about these representations which they are already aware about. She tries to involve the power of visualizing through the usage of rhyming words in many of these poems, which ideally help the readers to make these more relatable and memorable.

Words

They fill up our eyes,
They fill up our hearts,
They even take us miles apart!

They make you feel good,
And bad as it could,
And play every game, to be misunderstood!

Those Rhymes for Christmas,
Or Whines and Whispers,
Breaking you into relentless laughter!

They teach us love,
They teach us hate,
And teaches wisdom that's never too late!

They make us grieve,
They make us believe,
As days and nights, take our leave!

They come as sermons,
And warns as lessons,
At times creating lasting impressions!

Some are to treasure,
Some cause displeasure,

Some play with us, during their leisure!

We give them a tone,
We give them a voice,
We give them the power to make us feel nice!

Nature

Blue skies and blossoms,
Soft winds and seasons,
Raindrops and sunshine,
Just nature's realm, or even mine?

Sun-kissed roofs and rainbows,
Sunny days and mangoes,
Pathways and funny scarecrows,
Do they also twin my shadows?

A paradise to the lovers,
A palette to the artists,
A fantasy to all dreamers,
An antidote to mood shifts?

Wetlands and those forests,
Windstorms and lovely sunsets,
Farmlands and grassy pastures,
Simple and profound joys of nature!

A home to the flora 'n' fauna,
One that could never be enough,
Nurture their secrets; it's tough,
Sooner than the insatiable humans engulf!

Life

Why don't you take a minute or two?
Forgetting all those bruises and blues,
For life's a garden where you wither and bloom,
At times in peace, and at times in gloom.

It comes from earth and returns to earth,
Confusing man all the way from birth,
Get through the rains and you earn rainbows,
Just as that little joy, amidst your sorrows.

We're all gifted with the same days and nights,
Yet none of us ever get it right,
We take pride in holding on to our ropes tight,
While you are born to be happy and take it light!

Some say we take births again,
And none of our efforts go in vain,
Does one or more still matter,
More than how we let it all shatter?

Some deal it with an ounce of intelligence,
And some mess up with a bit of negligence,
It doesn't come with a manual or notes,
You get to build a paradise or a castle of hopes!

Wealth

Your possessions; may they be silver or gold,
Expensive closets or the wine that is old,
Mansions or Limos to give off those cues,
That life is extraordinary amidst all blues.

The title at work and those hefty perks,
Designer jewellery or those antique artworks,
Might make you feel rich and out of the world,
Are they real wealth, or are you in a dream
world?

Money and power, or rising to fame,
Or simple living without anyone to blame?
Coveted degrees or opulent looks,
Or wisdom from life, and not just from books!

Unending parties and exotic vacations,
Or just a beautiful bunch of carnations?
Seven-course dinners and signature king beds,
Or sharing candy and a snuggle with your kids?

VIP health checks and a day full of diets,
Or a walk in the nature, that keeps you quiet?
Latest tech gadgets and over-filled wallets,
Or a healthy small clan with just grateful hearts?

Wealth keeps you rich and happy for life,
But it's not just bucks, hope you get it right,
Knowledge is wealth, so is Wisdom,
Patience is wealth, so is Good Health,
Family is wealth, so are Friendships,
Respect is wealth, so is Honour,
Happiness is wealth, so are Memories,
Love is wealth too, and to be loved,
God is great wealth, and so are you too!

Relationships

Reach out to people
If they crossed your minds
Time is too little
For being unkind!

Shout out to those souls
For being our light
Thank them and love them
And hug them a bit tight!

You might sound crazy
For laughing out loud
Still take it easy
And stand out from the crowd!

Stop looking for magic
To work on your feelings
Start taking action
At times, with no logic!

Call them and wish them
Before they are gone
All we might take back
Are some memories or none!

Mother

The only one who can't see you quiet,
The only one who won't let you diet,
The only one who never feels right,
When it comes to their children's plight!

Those exam nights or stage frights,
She really knows how to get them right,
Beauty tips or boredom tricks,
She has choices that are hard to pick!

Lazy mornings or late-night shows,
Gets you whacks wherever you go,
Household chores or office deals,
Never takes her off her wheels!

The first to wake and last to snooze,
Forever engaged without excuse,
Missing socks or school supplies,
Always found only with her eyes!

She preps you up for all setbacks,
The first one there, to get your back,
She is your friend, and also your guide,
Always by your side and beaming with pride!

You argue and you smirk within,
Not knowing she lets you win,
You try and hide your flaws and falls,
Never to get she knows them all!

She needs no roses or sweet pies,
Nor those praises soaring her high,
Value her and hug her tight,
When you know she is mostly right!

You love superheroes who guard you at play,
You have a special one just a call away,
She does not have a cape or a wand,
But ties you in an eternal bond!

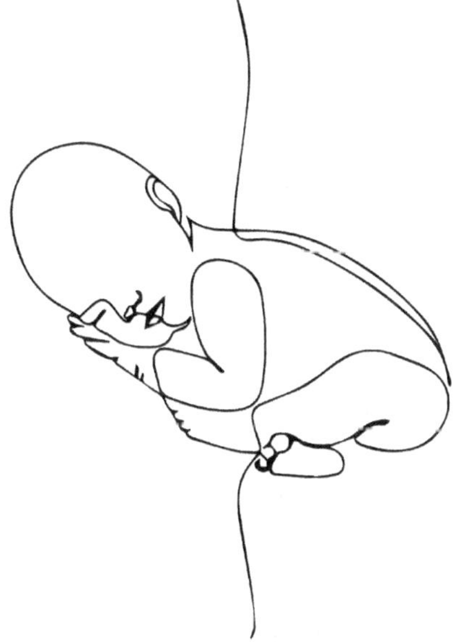

Father

He didn't get it soon as mom,
Until he saw your charming form,
You never grew big in his tummy,
Still you expect him to be brave as mummy?

He had never changed nappies before,
And knew you woke up with his snores,
Yet got you the best cradle in town,
And adored you in ways unknown!

He did not put on that extra weight,
But can you guess his heart beat rate?
Until he saw you and mom all fine,
Thanking and praying to the divine!

Sleepless nights and tiring drives,
Never stopped him to miss your smiles,
The day he held you in his hand,
Tears rolled down; no it wasn't planned!

He always saves up for your gifts,

Forgetting his own tiny wish list,
Until mom advises him to live a bit,
And reminds that he too is an eternal gift!

He too has his ups and downs,
But mostly handles everyone's frowns,
He still wishes to be that little boy again,
Free from stress and all such pains!

You share his watches,
And some of his clothes,
Or you are that pet daughter,
Who gets him on to laughter!

You don't get to choose them,
And you might not always like them,
Fathers may seem different,
Just try loving them upfront!

Children

They bring us hope,
They bring us joy,
They bring us love; be a girl or boy!

They love to play,
All night and day,
We still pay heed to all what they say!

They hear us talk,
They watch us act,
Do we raise them up, to be a copycat?

They steal a few candies,
They steal a few tarts,
Nothing bigger than our hearts!

They make us proud,
Whenever around,
Be it home or schoolground!

We teach them prudence,
They teach us patience,
God sends them as blessings in abundance!

School

It makes you go back to your
past,
It always has memories that last, 
Some which you regret and some
that you love,
Some more that took you a few feet above!

Never knew anyone who loved homeworks,
Nor someone who enjoyed surprise tests,
Unless you were that teacher's pet,
And always wanted to prove you were the best!

Those endless morn and night playthroughs,
And alarm clocks that went on snooze,
Those tucked-in shirts and polished shoes,
Never did change or let you choose!

No restaurant can give us such a taste,
Of that lunch box dish we just snatched and ate,
Recess and games kept pulling us back,
From those heavy and humongous backpacks!

Nothing seemed to make your day,
Like the striking bell end of the day,
Assembly lines and punishment fines,
Turned out to be our future lifelines!

Gratitude

The sunlight and the misty breeze,
The moonlit night putting you at ease,
The magpies and the rainbow skies,
Don't they bring you infinite peace?

The meals on time and mid-meal treats,
The play-dough sets and the lego streets,
The cartoon reels and midnight squeals,
Aren't these your magic pills?

A coffee mug that's hot and full,
That birdie by your window sill,
Cosy rugs and fancy quills,
Don't they make you fresh and full?

Messy homes and boring chores,
Holiday planning on the shores,
Busier days and awful plights,
Don't they keep us tucked in tight?

Thank the universe and your stars,
Thank your scars and the farce,
Thank the smiles, and countless breaths,
That makes our lives more precious than death!

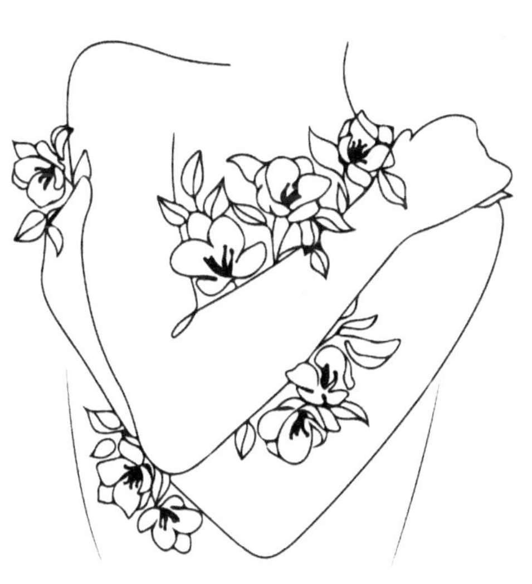

Professions

There is no right one, or one that's wrong,
As long as you totally belong,
You pour in some love and lots of passion,
And never fail to take the right action.

It's a means to life for some,
It means the complete life for some,
Some hate it and can't wait for the day to end,
Some are grateful for all the time they spend!

Some earn it the real hard way,
Some still treat it as child's play,
Some are proudly known for it,
And some are never made for it!

Some find delight in what they do,
Some can't find a single clue,
Some are born to adorn that seat,
Some quickly accept their defeat.

Some do their best, and leave the rest,
When luck and fortune give their own tests!
Some voice their pains and fight for rights,
And reclaim their lives without regrets.

Hold on to it without much worry,
If it loves you back and keeps you nourished,
Cut down the ties and better release,
If your worth is questioned, and leave you
buried.

Compromises

Those roads you take,
And vows you make,
Those hands you shake,
With dollars at stake.
Those roses you steal,
And hearts you heal,
Those lips you seal,
To strike a deal!
How happy does it seem,
To stand by a dream,
And help them redeem,
The ways of the Supreme!
Do eyes and minds see?
Or you fake a glee?
Or you guarantee?
To set your mind free?

Emotions

They just come and go as guests,
Some leave soon, and some give us tests,
We entertain how they make us feel,
On their own, they don't make a big deal!

You give them names and pick their shades,
You love them more and present with grades,
You obey them more than your brainwaves,
We aren't even aware we've become their slaves!

Not all of them take us to doom,
Some make us glow and some make us bloom,
Some are true and help us grow,
Some are known to steal the show!

They are valid, but at times deceptive,
They don't have a real objective,
You hide them with a smile or let them hover,
You better be in control, or they will take over!

They cannot be seen or touched,
They feel through us and seem bewitched,
We are familiar and made up of them,
Why still unapologetic about their outcomes?

Can't we be aware and responsible for them
Than flaunting them like some precious gem?
Blessed are those who treat them right,
Else your wisdom loses all its might!

Music

Soothing to our ears,
Often brings you tears,
Be it in a group or solo,
Mostly gets you cheers!

It could be your voice,
Or a few bagpipes,
Pitches or high notes,
Always gets you votes!

Culture or Science,
Artform or disguise,
Pop and rhythm and blues,
You've choices that confuse!

They play with our emotions,
While fostering connections,
Fiddling with notations,
Designing great creations!

There is one for all,
Healing big or small,
Opera or ballet hall,
Stay soulful and recall!

Eyes

They talk before you speak,
They hold the world you seek,
They love the way you sneak,
And build a bond so deep!

They bring out the best in you,
Also your vanquishing views,
They bring the truth forefront,
While you meet them and confront!

They hold some tales of pain,
Also few dreams in vain,
They make you look cheerful,
In a world that's so fearful!

You lose yourself in them,
You feel some souls through them,
They sing stories untold,
Like petite petals unfold!

They bring magic into everyday life,
And flaunt the beauty of a sapphire slice,
They reveal the poetry of the heart,
And are just living works of art!

Stories

They bring us joy,
They make us cry,
They even prompt us to think or to try!

Some make you eager,
Some bring in anger,
Some even make us feel superior!

Mystery or magic,
Or end up a bit tragic,
Some are romantic, or too dramatic!

Morals and musings,
Fables and fiction,
All of them bring out unique reactions!

Enjoyed at bed-time,
Even at tea-time,
Why don't you make it your favourite pass time?

Grandmas excel in them,
And we dwell on them,
They are too special and nothing short of a gem!

Self-Talk

What is it that makes you more 'efficient'?
Is it your will, or ideals that trend?
Is it a skill, or is it a scheme?
Or a lost and lonely midnight dream?

What is it that makes you feel 'successful'?
Is it a pocket that is so full?
Is it that job, or the name, or the fame?
Or just loving life, having no one to blame?

What is it that makes you feel 'beautiful'?
Is it those praises that take you higher?
Is it your jeweller, or funky hair-dryers ?
Or mirroring your worth, and staying bountiful?

What is it that makes you feel 'confident'?
Is it that pay cheque, or knowledge from books?
That big and bold title, or those deceitful looks?
Or being yourself; and always delighted?

What is it that makes you feel 'guilty'?
Those incomplete chores and daily deadlines?
Those unhealthy days and unsettling times?
Or worthy self-talks, and tranquillity?

Regrets

They come from actions and from inactions,
They break a person, bringing forth reasons,
Questioning choices, listing out advices,
Constantly making you guilty of vices!

Some live a life full of them,
Some realize it's not only about them,
Some bring it up every now and then,
Some do not care about it very often.

Some still wish to go back in time,
And try a hand at it one more time,
Conscious to pick and choose a line,
Or find out ways to simply mime!

Not every choice might be right,
Not all remedies save our plight,
Not all losses are worth your stress
And not all the wins are champion-like!

Train your minds to embrace more,
And your hearts to judge them less,
Don't lose hope in chasing the good,
Love your life and stay mindful!

Beauty

In the laugh of a child,
On the lap of the wild,
In a flower and a weed,
On the sprout of a seed,
In the elegance of a lady,
In the wilderness of a poppy,
In the colours of a macaw,
In the puzzles of a jigsaw,
In the vigour of a lad,
In the figure of a speech,
In the depth of an ocean,
In the rhythm of a notation,
In the eyes of a baby,
In the ways of a granny,
In the hands of an artist,
In the voice of the flautist,
In a bee in the garden,
In a heart that will pardon,
Don't you miss the beauty,
That makes our lives so worthy!

Coincidence

The regular bus that came in late,
That last one on the cookie plate,
Didn't they still help you and wait?
When all you did was wake up late!

The strike which happened at the gate,
Cancelling meetings on that date,
Didn't that still serve as a boon?
Coz' you could rest from morn to noon!

That abrupt call or note you got,
From the very same one you missed a lot,
That surprise good luck wish from dad,
Didn't they make you a lot more glad?

That good old friend who takes your blame,
Finding your name on a wall of fame,
Showers of rain on a scorching day,
Don't they take your breath away?

That train you booked and never took,
Those wedding chimes that never shook,
Hook with strangers hardly known,
By sheer luck, or vibes unknown?

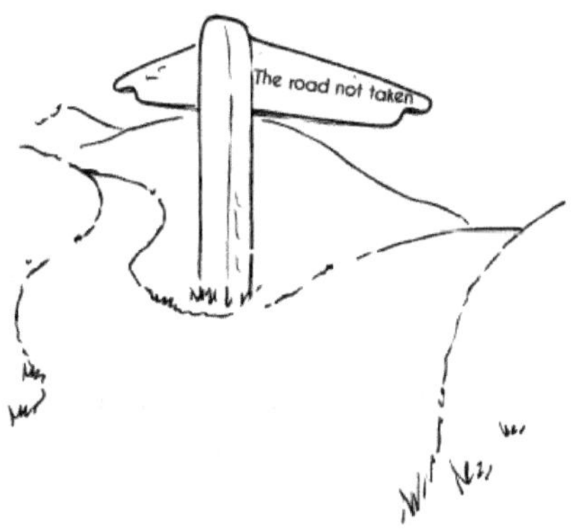
The road not taken

Wishes for my best-half

Valentine's wishes and candlelight dinners,
You taught that's not what love is all about,
Painted skin and perfect bodies,
You knew that's not love, without a doubt!

The mundane chores or dishes undone,
Never annoy you, or stopped our fun,
Days and nights have never been hasty,
All that you ever need is a cup of hot tea!

You love to see me bloom and glow,
And never try to steal the show,
I stay at home, or love to work
You are always the best, never to irk!

The best long drives or workplace stints,
Keeps you cool without a hint,
Weekend treats or wardrobe buys,
You love my choice and opt for me to try!

We love and fight together, we know,
You have never given me a no,
Annoying you for the rest of your life,
Life-long memories from your extraordinary
wife! :)

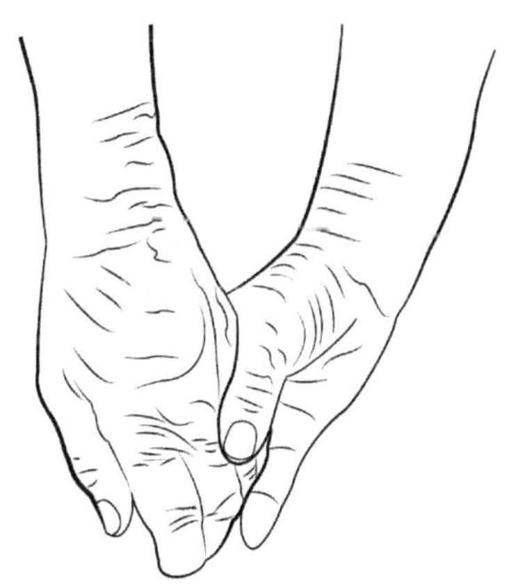

Silence

I bring you waves of peace,
And put your mind at ease,
Thoughts work well with me,
When words fail to speak!

I escort boredom to the classrooms,
I help two parties not to fume,
I adorn the beautiful bride in florals,
And hide your pain and grief at funerals!

I guard their dreams when your little ones
snooze,
And channel your pleas to the Gods you choose,
I guide the life of a monk by the riverside,
And leave the virtues of hell terrified!

I'm always welcomed at most of the places,
I leave all venues without any traces,
I love my restrained roles in romance,
And leave the mystic audience in trance!

I foster fear in nasty courtrooms,
And future dreams in lofty boardrooms,
I grace events of ceremonial homage,
And need no command of a specific language!

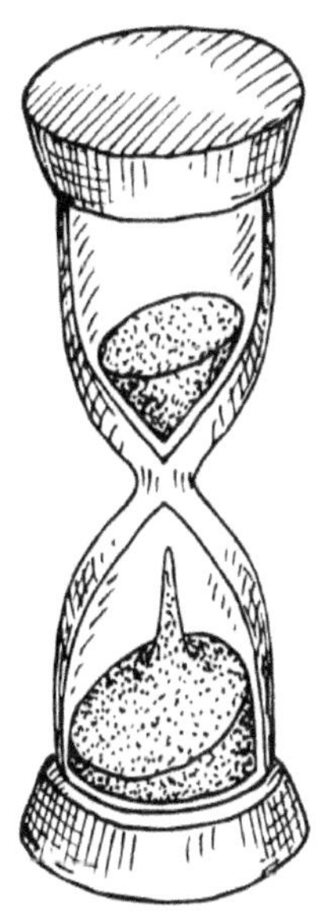

Our Inner Monsters

Waiting for attention,
Working in exhaustion,
Fuming with aggression,
Leaves with what impression?

Dealing with depression,
Harming with deception,
Failing with obsessions,
Are these your possessions?

Fuming with jealousy,
Dreaded by apathy,
Handcuffed by insecurity,
Banging on self-pity?

Coping with conflicts,
Living with hard guilt,
Thriving in anger,
Pushing self to danger?

It is poison in itself,
Being a threat to thyself,
No vampires play closer,
With these real inner monsters!

Art

It is in the way you speak,
It is in the way you care,
It is in the way you dress,
Also how you handle distress!

It is in the way you smile,
It is in the way you love,
It is in the way you dream,
Also in ways you believe!

It is in the roads you take,
It is in the food you make,
It is in the books you like,
Also in the way you thank!

It is how you keep your home,
It is how you use your tone,
It is how you hear and see,
Even how you make your tea!

It is how you paint your real world,
It is how you hum to your own pains,
It is how you dance your plight away,
And how you made you proud all day!

Kindness

You need it at work,
You need it in schools,
You need it with humans,
 And all creatures too!

It takes out your stress,
And brings in some love,
It gets you a bow,
And takes you above!

You get it with birth,
Or with time on this earth,
It keeps you in bliss,
Dare not to miss!

You feel it through words,
You see it through deeds,
You sense it from souls,
Who practice with ease!

Solitude

I love my cup of coffee alone,
And to sit by the radio even at noon,
I find it healthy and very soothing,
To spend my own time engaging.

It doesn't pain me being alone,
Always for reasons unknown,
I can hear my inner voice,
Away from all the unwanted noise.

I don't expect anyone to accompany,
I bet it; I like my own company,
Sparkling rivers or setting sun
They all embrace us, their loved ones!

My happiness truly matters the most,
There is nothing else to boast,
It makes me beautiful, and I adore,
That it helps me always find my core.

It truly helps me embrace my soul,
And brings in freedom on the whole,
I grow beyond my body and mind,
When mystic spiritual vibes unwind!

Spirituality

Some owe it to their scars,
Some still believe in their stars,
Some use it as their shield,
Some trust it when they're healed!

Some try to seek it,
Some others create it,
Some try to teach their soul,
Some try to see it in all.

It takes good faith to choose a path,
Helps a bit, if you are a natural empath,
Illusions and learnings come your way,
Keeping feelings and emotions at bay.

Some make complete sense out of it,
Few still get away making fun of it,
It connects us with a higher self,
Not when you are focused only on yourself!

It is divinely pure and not corrupt,
The way to it is always in your heart,
You get to take charge of your ego,
Be grateful and just let it go!

We start to look past ourselves,
Realising life's truly arduous,
The journey to within feels less tiring,
By just embracing a soul, that's enlightening.

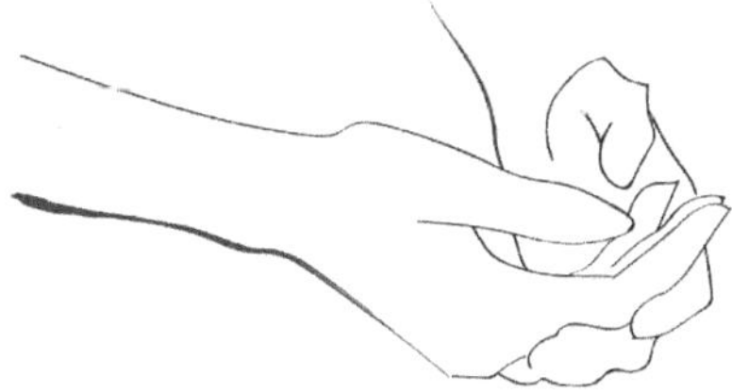

Love

Love can never treat you wrong,
You better discover where you belong,
No one can take it away,
It's only a heartbeat away!

Roses bring love, rainbows bring love,
Love yourself first, rest all comes next.
Children bring love, candies bring love,
Love matters most, when you're at your best.

Poets try a hand,
Still none gets it right,
You can't have it planned,
It's well out of your sight.

Love makes you grow,
Love makes you glow,
Love ties you down,
And makes you bow down.

Love gives you peace,
Lets you live with ease,
Or tears you apart,
Even if you're smart!

Some carry joy,

Some only destroy,
Some bring us grief,
Some teach us belief.

Some are bound to last,
Some get us into the past,
Some are calm and quiet,
Some meant to stay upright,

You have it in just words,
And not once in your deeds,
Fails both you and that one,
You lose a gem unknown!

Love is not sex or going on dates,
Love is that light you see in someone's eyes.
Love is that confidence that you are enough.
Love is that commonness of not being tough.

Love is making sure you're okay,
Every night and every day,
Love is that calming and confirming voice,
Holding you up even while you aren't so nice!

Caterpillar to Butterfly

She was never addressed as pretty,
Or for that matter even brainy,
Cause it was never just about her,
But always weighed against someone other!

She always felt lost and lonely,
Even amidst a complete family,
Classmates named her nerd and bossy,
Cause she was different and a bit choosy!

Mom could never be at her best,
She had to fix her own life first!
Dad was almost out of sight,
Grandma chose to raise her right!

She always longed for hugs and cuddles,
Could never find them even in riddles,
Siblings could share and bring some fun,
Thankfully God had sent her one!

She always had to bear the cross,
To get everyone's lives across,
She always wished to have some fun,
At home and work, but had no one.

True love took turns to change her life,
And held her hand promising a fair life,
Life never crawled, but played with clues
Bringing worth and peace, and endless hues!

Moments of Death

Someone loved being gone,
Finding no worth being born,
Proving oneself on and on,
Wishing you could just move on!

That unfulfilled day-dream,
That love you didn't redeem,
Those hushed-up scary screams,
Bringing up true life unseen!

Being a coward all the time,
Not voicing what's not fine,
Not growing up with pride,
Life still gives few a jolly ride!

Those endless fights for equity,
Being treated without quality,
Forced to accept the harsh reality,
Still surviving post-brutality!

It's not just about your steady breaths,
But also the moments which show their depth,
A gift is often termed a present,
For life's to be lived today, and not to resent!

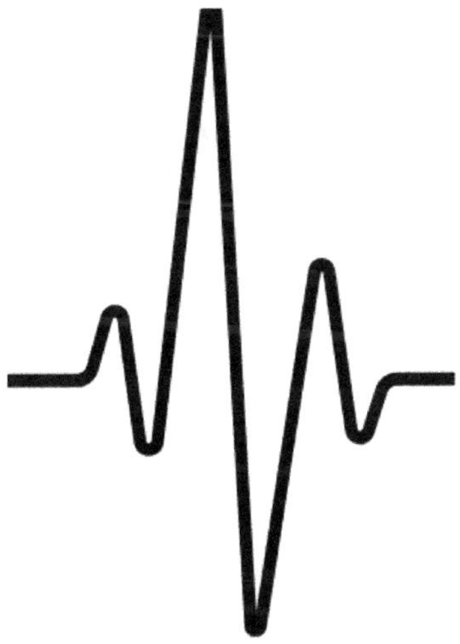

www.ingramcontent.com/pod-product-compliance
Lightning Source LLC
LaVergne TN
LVHW021238200726

843509LV00012B/1527